Download The Au
Of This Book

If you love listening to audiobooks on- ᴏɪ enjoy the
narration as you read along, I have great news for you. You can
download the audio book version of

HYGGE
THE DANISH SECRETS OF HAPPINESS:
HOW TO BE HAPPY AND HEALTHY IN
YOUR DAILY LIFE

for FREE just by signing up for a FREE 30-day audible trial.
Just scan or use the links below:

For Audible UK:

https://tinyurl.com/y2sc5mvl

For Audible US:

https://tinyurl.com/y6xhclbu

REVIEWS

Reviews and feedback help improve this book and the author. If you enjoy this book, we would greatly appreciate it if you could take a few moments to share your opinion and post a review on Amazon.

FREE BONUS

HYGGE GIFT IDEAS

Go to https://mailchi.mp/752b5b4dd620/mayathoresen to download the guide for free

HYGGE

The Danish Secrets of Happiness: How to Be Happy and Healthy in Your Daily Life

Maya Thoresen

ISBN: 9781671190832

Contents

CHAPTER 1:

WHAT IS HYGGE?

Have you ever heard of hygge? This word is synonymous with coziness and comfort, but many people are currently unfamiliar with its use. In essence, hygge refers to a concept that is deeply rooted in Danish and Norwegian culture. As it is a cultural norm in Scandinavia, it might explain why people in this area experience a higher quality of living than other cultures. Hygge is linguistically versatile and can be used to refer to all aspects of life in the form of a noun, verb, or adjective.

If you were to ask a Danish person precisely what hygge means, he or she would clarify that it doesn't mean just one concept. Instead, there are numerous elements that comprise this way of living, and you may already be doing some of them unknowingly period. Although there is no true English translation of the word, the best connotations that come to mind when thinking about "hygge" include "cozy," "warm," "contentedness," "comfort," "togetherness," and "relaxation." However, these impressions only begin to skim the surface of a much broader concept.

As far as its practical implications, hygge is extremely useful for self-care as well as tending to both the mind and body in the cold winter months. Many scholars believe that is how the concept began: It made the winter more bearable and comfortable for the early Scandinavians.

Hygge has, however, transformed into a worldwide trend that has been gaining popularity in the last few years because of its simplicity and its adherence to the trend of minimalism. Often, Westerners complain about busy lives in which they never stop moving, so applying hygge concepts to their daily practices can improve their overall lifestyles. By integrating some of the hygge principles into daily routine, one can greatly improve their overall level of happiness.

IS HYGGE A GOOD FIT FOR YOU?

You may find yourself wondering whether or not hygge is the right for you. After all, it might sound difficult to make so many changes in your life at once, or maybe you think you're not the kind of person who can really do something that drastic. But as long as you're looking for a way to reduce clutter and ease your mind a little too, hygge is the perfect fit for you!

Specifically, hygge can work for individuals, couples, families, and anyone who wants to feel better and more mindful of their experiences. Another way to determine whether or not hygge is right for you is to consider what makes someone more receptive to living the hygge way. To contemplate if the hygge lifestyle is right for you, try asking yourself these key questions:

* Am I stressed out by normal, everyday life? **There are many ways to deal with the stress of daily life. For many who give it a try, hygge can help reduce the overall sense of stress and emotional and psychological trouble. Practicing a hygge lifestyle helps you slow down and take everything one step at a time. It also helps you live in the moment and enjoy the time you spend doing the things you love, so you feel more capable of dealing with the things you may not like so much.**

* Do I feel like I need to recharge my mind? **Hygge can be a great way to recharge mentally. Keep in mind that hygge is about staying in the present and practicing mindfulness as much as possible. For this reason, keeping hygge in your heart can enable your mind to feel more rested and recharged more often, too. If you feel overwhelmed all the time by the events and people around you, be sure to take some time for mindfulness as well as self-care. These proactive measures can make a big difference in improving your feelings daily. They also increase your emotional and mental resilience.**

- Do I have trouble coping with changes or problems? Both can be scary, and while some people are able to address these situations with dignity and ease, others may lack coping mechanisms, causing stress and panic. If you're someone who isn't sure how to deal with uncertainty or pressure, hygge can assist you. By remaining mindful and taking care of yourself and your feelings, you can use hygge to feel better about problems that may arise. Although you may not be able to completely solve every issue with hygge, it's a great tool to help you feel calmer in the face of adversity.

- Am I always thinking about money, work, or some other stressful part of my life? Bring hygge into your finances, your job, your romantic relationship, your family, and any other part of your life that may be causing you to feel overwhelmed. The more you focus on a source of stress—like work, for example—the more it consumes you and keeps you from living your best life. When you allow hygge to influence your life instead, you will be able to work through these kinds of daunting issues more effectively. Hygge can allow you to feel comfortable and safe even when you're dealing with dilemmas and chaos in other aspects of your life.

- Do I want less clutter? If so, hygge may be a perfect solution for you. This lifestyle is all about reducing clutter and keeping things as minimal as possible. Although you do not have to give up everything for hygge, you should be willing and able to abandon a little bit here and there to make your life less cluttered and confusing overall. You'll use minimalistic furnishings and items in your home when you live the hygge way, and you won't keep a bunch of unnecessary junk. The more you work on downsizing, the more organized your home and life will become. Engaging in this practice can help you feel calm and more hygge than ever before!

- Do I feel like I never have a chance to take care of myself? Self-care is a big part of hygge, so if you're worried about not being able to take care of your own feelings and needs, this lifestyle may work well for you. However, it's important to remember that hygge is not about putting yourself first. Instead, it is about making equal time for yourself and for everyone important in your life, too. Don't neglect your friends and family in favor of your own needs, but don't abandon your own needs either. Finding the right balance will help you feel at ease and will improve your hygge experience.

- Do I value things that are comfortable and cozy? If you love to be physically comfortable and surrounded by things with soft, pleasant textures, hygge is definitely the lifestyle for you. Hygge is about making sure you have both sensory and aesthetic comfort available to you at all times. To illustrate, decorating with soft, comfortable fabrics and gentle lines and textures throughout your home is a major part of hygge– though it's important not to overdo the décor, or spend too much money on it, either. Keep things simple and easy when you decorate, and you'll be able to enjoy that comfort even more in no time.

- Would it be nice to have more time for the things and people I care about? Sometimes, it may feel like you can't make enough time for your friends, your romantic partner, your colleagues, or your kids. No matter what you try to do, does it seem like someone is always excluded from your plans? If you feel this way frequently, you may need to try regrouping with hygge. Hygge can help you organize your time better and make sure everyone you care about is getting an equal share of your energy and time. You can also spend time being comfortable and cozy with the people you care about to improve your hygge experience as well.

Of course, these questions really only start to explore the reasons why you may be interested in hygge. Just keep them in mind while you're trying to figure out whether or not this lifestyle is conducive for you. Hygge is very forgiving, so if you try it and find that it doesn't work for you, there's no reason to feel discouraged or guilty. This attempt just means you haven't found the right lifestyle plan yet, and that's okay!

WHY COZINESS?

What is it about being cozy that makes it such a valuable feeling, and such an integral part of hygge? Coziness helps you feel comfortable and safe. This feeling encourages you to slow down, to consider your experiences and surroundings, and to take time for yourself while also giving your time to others. When you're cozy, you're more likely to be happy, content, and at peace with yourself and the world around you. Practicing hygge will help you increase your coziness in no time.

But is it really that easy to be cozy? Is it beneficial to try practicing such a lifestyle when the world around you is so hectic? Many people believe trying to be cozy and comfortable in all aspects of life is futile. Critics feel that taking too much time to relax will prevent individuals from being ready to face problems and situations that might arise in their day to day lives. These critics insist that hygge practitioners will be unprepared for the twists and turns of life if they're too busy taking care of themselves to pay attention to the stressful world around them.

However, practicing hygge and coziness does not imply that you're unprepared or not paying attention to the world around you. In fact, being cozy and relaxed can help you better face problems when they do arise. In essence, hygge can help make it easier for you to cope when things go badly. The more comfortable you are during the good times, the more rested your brain will be when it needs to address problems. You'll also be able to heal emotionally from life's inevitable stresses when you practice a cozy lifestyle, too.

There are many reasons why you might want to incorporate coziness into your life. There's more to it than just being comfortable, and you may be able to find new ways to face life in all its forms when you make hygge a key part of your regular lifestyle.

CHAPTER 2:
HYGGE
PRINCIPLES

So far, you have gotten a glimpse of how you can incorporate the Danish way of hygge into your life in diverse ways, all of which you will learn more about throughout this book. The simplest way to begin is by engaging the basic principles of hygge, which are the primary foundations of the lifestyle. Once you grasp these tenets, you will be well on your way to implementing them in your life, and therefore, on your way to improved health and happiness!

1. MINDFULNESS AND THE SENSES

Mindfulness may be the hardest principle on the list, yet it is one of the most important to cultivate your true happiness through this practice. Mindfulness means you are paying attention to the moment. You are fully engaged in whatever activity you are immersed within presently.

Here are some common situations in which you can practice being more mindful of what you're doing:

- Watching a movie

- Reading a book

- Having a conversation with a friend

- Drinking a cup of tea

Mindfulness refers to any moment in your life where you are absorbed in the moment, enjoying yourself, and not worrying about the past or the future. Think of it as the adage, «Stop and smell the roses!»

In the chaotic and fast-paced modern world, many of us forget to enjoy the moment because we are so busy thinking about that deadline we have to meet or the groceries we have to pick up for the week. Hygge encourages you to change this behavior. Let the aroma of a cup of coffee reach your nose before you take a sip. Enjoy the intricacies and colors of your loved one's eyes, and notice how soft your cotton sweater feels against your skin. Combining your attention without distractions with a full sensory experience helps you slow down the clock and enjoy your time. These seemingly simple moments also help you create cherished memories you can reflect upon later.

Mindfulness is a habit you must develop over time. You can't expect yourself to always be mindful; you have to constantly work on it. One great way to achieve mindfulness is to simply stop what you are doing a minute or two each day and savor the world around you. Take this time to breathe in deeply and truly process what you're seeing, hearing, feeling, and doing. When you are engrossed in a task and realize your mind is wandering, pull it back to the present. Redirect your thoughts to the present moment until it becomes a habit for you to think in this manner.

2. GRATITUDE AND BEING POSITIVE

It may seem like common sense that looking at the positive side of things would make us feel happier, but that doesn't mean it is an easy practice. In fact, we may not even realize that we are being negative sometimes.

The first rule of bringing positivity into your daily life is feeling and expressing gratitude. When was the last time you told someone you appreciate them, or thanked them for opening the door or helping you with the dishes? These are the little things we often forget, and it can make our days brighter because we are making someone else happy when we express gratitude. When we feel grateful for something, we are also feeding on the positive flow of energy from the person we have thanked. A simple show of thanks can go a long way, especially if someone has had a horrible day.

The next step in positivity is about finding that bright spot in the darkness. There is no denying that this world is a chaotic one that can sometimes lead to heartache. Fortunately, you can often find something good in your life on which to focus, even in the worst circumstances.

Think and act positively in all you do. Choose to talk about the good things instead of complaining. Look for sources of good news instead of overwhelming yourself and feeling down about all the tragedies around the world. It is important to be informed, but not to the point that you feel depressed due to dark and gloomy headlines. You do not have to think about bad news 24/7 to stay in touch with what's happening globally and locally.

3. NATURE

If you know anything about the Nords and their traditions, you saw this one coming. Being active in nature is not only calming but also inspiring. Nature is what we come from, physically and spiritually. Even if modern conveniences make our lives easier, there is still a part within each of us that summons the wild. Nature is a great way to practice using all your senses as well. Smelling flowers, feeling the cold chill of the wind on your cheek, listening to birds singing, and seeing the bright colors of spring can inspire anyone's appreciation and encourage them to love the world around him or her.

It is important to incorporate nature into your life. Here are a few easy suggestions to accomplish this goal:

- Go on a hike.

- Visit the beach.

- Keep potted plants in your home or on your patio.

- Work in the garden.

- Spend time sitting outside, even if you're just relaxing.

- Bring your family members, pets, friends, or colleagues along for these outside excursions.

4. EASE AND COMFORT

This is something that can easily be expressed through what you wear or how things are done in your home. **One of the words used to describe the word hygge is "cozy," and that is what you are trying to achieve. Surround yourself with things that bring you comfort and warmth.**

Try these ideas for keeping things comfortable in your home and in your life:

- Use pillows that are soft, comfortable, and minimalistic, instead of flashy and impractical ones.

- Wear your favorite sweatpants and a comfortable sweater for the day instead of dressing up.

- Go makeup-free when you feel like it.

- Keep soft slippers available for use indoors.

Remember, comfort and ease go hand-in-hand, so the comfortable choices you make should not be challenging or difficult ones.

Choose to abandon the discomforts of life if you can. Of course, you can't always avoid discomfort since it is an inevitable part of life, but sometimes you endure uncomfortable things because you choose to do so. You don't have to! If you have a pair of shoes that look nice but feel horrible, donate. You don't need to sacrifice comfort for temporary beauty.

If there is someone around you who makes you uncomfortable or radiates a negative presence, don't feel as if you have to keep this person in your life. If talking it over doesn't work, it's better to free yourself from that negativity and bad influence, and focus on the people who bring happiness and comfort to your life. You should evaluate people that you don't like or don't want to be around, and remove them if you can.

Making life easier does *not* make you lazy; it makes you smart. If you find a way to streamline work or automate your technology, then do so. You are busy and tired enough—why add stress to your life by doing things the hard way? Remember, comfort and ease are important factors in your new lifestyle.

5. TOGETHERNESS

The Danish believe in spending quality time with one another. Friends and loved ones should take up a good portion of your time, even if it feels difficult to make time in your busy schedule. Don't you feel better after a cup of coffee with your best friend or a Netflix night with your spouse? There is a reason for that. We are all connected, and we are all meant to complement one another. You cannot have true happiness without taking advantage of companionship.

One of the major principles of this time spent with those you care for relates back to mindfulness. It means giving your full attention to the people that you are with currently. Cell phones and other distractions can keep you distant and only allow you to experience part of the moment. These should be set aside in favor of conversations and physical closeness. Stop letting insignificant distractions get in the way of truly being there with your loved ones.

Remember that none of us live forever, so appreciate the people you love while they are still here. Although this mentality may seem morbid, focus on how you can enjoy your time with loved ones instead of the limitations of time. Be mindful and stay in the moment with them, avoiding both internal and external distractions.

There are many lesser problems we may face, even without worrying about death. Plenty of us are taught to keep our problems to ourselves. We don't want to burden other people with the things that bother or distress us. We feel like an annoyance when we are upset or have a problem. But hygge encourages you to connect with the people you care for and with those who love you. Part of forging that connection involves reaching out to your family and friends when you need help. Talk to them and share what is bothering you. Form stronger bonds with them by letting them into your life, your mind, and your heart. You can't deal with life alone, and you will enjoy and appreciate having the support of these people by your side.

6. PLEASURE

Hygge is all about enjoying the simple pleasures of life. Can you honestly say that you do that regularly? You may take a vacation or two every year and make time for a fancy date night once a month, but hygge principles actually embody something even simpler than that. Hygge pleasure is about slowing down and enjoying the small things that you don't have to look far to find. This could be your favorite dessert, a walk along the beach with the feeling of sand in between your toes, or the laughter of your children as you tickle them. We need to learn to find these moments and make them happen. Pleasure in a hygge lifestyle is about the experience around us, instead of unexpected lavish gifts and large expensive events.

There are countless enjoyable moments around you all the time, but the majority of us fail to pay attention to them. One of life's little secrets is that the wealth and pleasure you work hard for and wait for is usually not what you expect. You could work relentlessly for a lavish vacation, only to have things go wrong and end up not enjoying the free time. You save up for months to buy that product you want, only to find that it doesn't work as well as you wanted. You work tirelessly at your job to increase your wealth, only to find that years have passed, and you don't have as much time to enjoy the fruits of your labor. When you put a desire on a pedestal and delay life in order to strive for it, it will evade you. It will never fail to disappoint. When you accept pleasure as something that surrounds you and something that you create consistently with your attitude, then you will find that pleasure is much more abundant and available than you think.

Again, pleasure does not require time, money, or other people. It requires a focus in attitude. You must be open to pleasure; you must accept it without trying to change it or control it. You must look for it in the world around you and be grateful for it when you find it. True joy lies in the little moments. Embrace those moments. You will get into the habit of finding them more and more throughout your day when you start to adopt the hygge attitude and lifestyle.

Of course, you don't have to lie back and wait for pleasure to come to you. You can deliberately create a more pleasant atmosphere and situations in your life. Hygge is something that can come naturally, but you can do many things to emphasize it and foster it in your life. If something brings you pleasure, why not add it to your life and boost your mood as a result?

8. MINIMALISM AND QUIET

Part of hygge is the belief that minimalism will bring you peace and happiness. This mentality applies for every facet of life, but especially in regards to your home décor. Having the bare minimum that you need in furniture with a simple layout, including a quiet corner to have some time alone to read or meditate, can make you feel less cluttered.

Excess amounts of stuff can stress you out and bog down your energy. You have too many things to worry about, organize, and clean. There is no need for so much clutter. Having a more minimal lifestyle allows you to breathe, both literally and metaphorically.

You might consider Swedish death cleaning. This type of cleaning is a decluttering method where you ask yourself, "What do I really need in my life?" It encourages you to remove excess things that you don't need. Consider how your loved ones will have to clean out your house when you pass away. The more unnecessary things you have, the more stress they will have to deal with upon your passing. You can minimize that potential stress by getting rid of the things you can absolutely live without or excesses that you no longer need. Let yourself be freer by omitting clutter.

If you can't let go of something for some sentimental reason, then keep it, but find clever ways to store these things. One option is to invest in a storage unit, put the items away, and give them some time to sit there. After a while of not living with the sentimental items and not seeing them, do you still want them? Or can you safely get rid of them, knowing you won't miss them?

Another tip is to hang your clothes backward. When you wear clothes and put them away again, hang them the right way. At the end of the year, if there are any clothes left that are still facing the wrong way, you know that you never wore them. You can probably get rid of them without regret now.

Consider donating things instead of throwing them away haphazardly. Remember the classic expression, "One man's trash is another man's treasure?" You might just make someone's day by giving him or her something for free or at an affordable price. The act of being kind to others can give you a warm sense of pleasure, which is all part of hygge.

POSSIBLE HYGGE PITFALLS

Although the principles listed above may sound easy, they can be more challenging than you may realize. Be aware of these potential mistakes and pitfalls that could hinder your hygge attempts:

- Spending too much time on yourself. Although helping yourself feel better and reducing stress in your own life is a big part of hygge, you should also make time for your friends, pets, colleagues, and family members. Hygge is about making yourself comfortable as well as increasing the comfort of those around you. It's also about learning to love yourself and others more, and about expressing that love and appreciation, too.

- Spending too much money. You may be tempted to throw out everything you own to replace it with more minimalistic furnishings and items, but that isn't very practical and can make you more stressed and anxious. If you're already trying to practice hygge on a budget, this can be even more upsetting and difficult. Even if you're not on a budget, there's no need to waste the items you already have. Instead, you may want to just remove some of the items in your home while keeping those you can use. Remember that hygge needs to be functional and practical to work.

- Unrealistic expectations. Hygge works slowly, over time, to improve your mood and help you feel good. It isn't going to immediately solve all your problems with your job, relationships, or life in general. Go into it expecting to work to achieve those goals, rather than looking for a magical fix. Even with lots of time, hygge may not solve every issue in your life. This concept is not meant to be a quick solution, but rather a lifestyle change that can help you learn to face problems and work through difficulties more easily. Be sure you're approaching hygge with a healthy mindset to get the most out of it.

Be on the lookout for these pitfalls when you first get started with hygge and later on in your practice, too. These issues can appear at any time throughout your hygge experience, but they can be easily avoided when you're prepared to potentially deal with them. If you're practicing hygge with others in your life, then you can help each other look out for signs of these hazards, too.

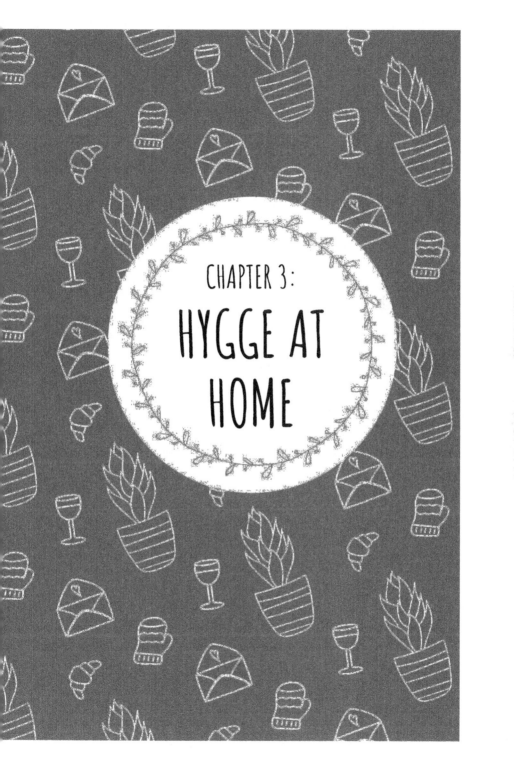

CHAPTER 3:
HYGGE AT HOME

Much of the hygge tradition is practiced within the home, so it stands to reason that you would need to change your home, at least a little, to reflect your new lifestyle. Happiness should be centered around the home as a place to relax with your friends and family. It is a precious sanctuary where you can unwind and be your authentic self. All of your worries and stresses need to be left at the door.

HYGGE DÉCOR

Hygge décor is simple. It is easy to incorporate into any home, and the décor itself is aesthetically pleasing. "Minimalism" and "simplicity" are the key terms in gauging how the hygge house should feel. Instead of creating a chaotic home that bogs you down with mess and induces stress with constant organizing and cleaning, try to simplify things. Often the most beautiful homes are designed by simplicity. Ever noticed how homes that are stuffed with things and clashing décor aren't necessarily pleasing to the eye?

At the same time, your home is a place that should bring you pleasure. Therefore, you want it to look a way that appeals to you. You want to fill it with things you enjoy looking at. You want to add items that give your home that special unique quality that says *you*.

Your home décor should also be useful and functional. A large glass figurine that is easy to break in a home with a lot of activity, for example, is impractical. Useless décor serves to be monetarily wasteful, and you could use that space for items you actually need and can utilize in daily activities.

Let's consider another example: If you love playing pool but find that you don't have room for a pool table because of your fancy coffee table, ask yourself, "Do I ever use that coffee table?" Replace the coffee table with the pool table and rearrange your furniture. Or maybe you have a sofa set with many pieces that makes it difficult to navigate the living room. Why not get rid of the couches you don't use and replace them with things like a bookshelf or a TV that you will actually use?

Go for décor that is simple and functional, preferably in light or warm colors. Pastels or warm colors are more cheerful than dark, depressing colors. Be sure everything that is meant for comfort is comfortable, and make use of texture. You can incorporate texture with pillows, blankets, rugs, and other accessories that make you feel great when you feel them between your fingers and toes. Remember to choose minimal, functional furnishings that feel soft and comfortable whenever possible.

Much of the best décor can be found in places such as Etsy, where many crafty individuals apply their talents and passion to create hygge items and accessories. Handmade items are often more comfortable, have a personal flair to them, and are pleasing to the eye. Plus, they add character to your home.

When it comes to making space in your home, you can go to The Container Store or order cute storage bins and shelves online. Store your stuff out of the way and keep it organized neatly. You can ensure that your storage is both attractive and functional. Having clutter everywhere to trip over is not attractive nor functional. It is far better to put things in proper places, as it will make your home inviting and easier to clean.

HYGGE AND ANIMALS

Did you know you can practice hygge through your pets, too? Pets can offer comfort and are calming. They're also cute. Pets often relieve stress and bring joy to your life. However, it's important to be sure you make the right pet decision for your household and your lifestyle.

For example, a snake may not be the best option if you are afraid of reptiles or do not know how to care for one. On the other hand, if you aren't afraid of them, and if you live in a small apartment or a place where you cannot have a more traditional pet, a snake, lizard, or frog may be perfect for you. A dog may not be ideal if you don't have time and will worry about it too much while you are at work. In contrast, if you have a big family with lots of people who can help care for it, then a dog may be the right choice.

Remember, too, that pets are a responsibility and can sometimes add to your daily stresses. Will you be willing and able to take care of the pet if it gets sick or injured? Would vet bills add to your stress about money? Will you be able to keep the pet for its whole natural lifespan? Consider all aspects of pet ownership before deciding to bring one home.

CREATING A HYGGE ATMOSPHERE

Hygge is all about how you feel, so even if you only have simple and comfortable furniture, this approach is a great start. Fill every room with something that makes you feel cozy. Try Egyptian cotton sheets on your bed, cashmere clothes for relaxing on the sofa, and scents in your bathroom that soothe and heal you, such as lavender. If you surround yourself with little things that make you feel good, you will soon find you are a much happier and healthier person on the inside.

Other items such as a drawing your child made at school, a sentimental treasure from your childhood, or stuffed animals are all things that you can add to each room to bring you that warm fuzzy feeling of being home. Sometimes, it is okay to sacrifice perfection and beauty for comfort. If you have something that doesn't quite match your home's theme, but still makes you happy, then show it off! You will be creating a conversation piece while lightening your mood when you are home.

As mentioned, creating a hygge lifestyle and atmosphere doesn't require you to go out and spend a fortune on new décor, especially if you don't have the budget for it. Any splurging will only increase your stress and defy the basic concept of hygge. Instead, use what you have, or buy small, inexpensive things. If you can, splurge on a few items that you absolutely love so you can have a few high-quality pieces that bring you comfort and joy. Just remember that you don't have to go on a huge shopping spree and spend money you don't have to make your home comfortable.

If your home makes you happy as it currently is, and if it is full of joy and cheer, then perhaps you don't need to change much or even anything at all—it is clearly perfect for your needs. But if your home depresses you, stresses you out, or embarrasses you in some way, it may be time for some changes. Your home environment impacts your mood significantly, so make it something you can enjoy living in and brings you comfort. You will notice an improvement in your life when you change your home to reflect who you truly are and what you like.

37

THE IMPORTANCE OF CANDLES

Imagine a time before electricity, when heat and light came from fires and candles. Danish winters are bitter cold, and hygge was as much of a necessity as it was something beautiful to hold onto in bleak times. Wrapping up in blankets and gathering around the fire or using candles to illuminate a room to tell stories or enjoy a delicious meal doesn't have to be a practice of the past. The warm glow of a candle, as well as the soothing scents you can find , can work wonders on your mood.

In hygge homes, you will find many candles lit year-round. Using candles is often the first step in creating a new hygge way of living as it is the most iconic piece of the puzzle. You can go with simple tea lights or find a beautiful candle with a scent that makes you feel relaxed. Find pretty candle holders that play with the light in attractive ways. You can also utilize small lamps and natural salt lamps to create a warm, romantic ambiance. The options are endless—it's up to you to discover what you like for your home and lifestyle!

HYGGE IN YOUR PERSONAL SPACE

Hygge is all about creating a personal space where you can leave your cares behind and simply enjoy the act of existing. Part of the hygge lifestyle is creating a personal space where you can become mindful and leave your stress, worry, and pain at the door. Your personal space does not have to be the whole house, especially if you share your house with other people. It can simply be a room or even a corner in a room. It is a small, comfortable space where you can be your authentic self. You can go there to recharge after a long day and engage in your hobbies.

Make your personal space uniquely yours. Decorate it however you want. Common features are pleasing aromas, comfortable furniture, cushy pillows, and lights that make you feel warm and at peace.

Remember that your personal space is just for you. You can expect to be left alone here. Tell others that if you are in your personal space, they should leave you be. Only invite in the people that bring you joy and make you feel good. Toxicity should stay at the door! Because you are using this space for relaxing, try to remove electronics and communication devices from the area. Let this space cradle you and melt away your worries. You don't need to be distracted by work when you are in your space, either. This is a peaceful place, so if you choose to read a book while you're there, choose something easy and light rather than a difficult or sad book.

Remember to use your personal space for what you enjoy doing. A personal space could be a craft room or a yoga studio. It could be a studio where you paint or an office where you write. If you love cooking, it could be your well-stocked kitchen where you create many culinary delights. It could be your man cave, where you watch football and enjoy a beer after work. It could simply be your half of the bed, where you meditate and write in your journal before you go to sleep. Just make sure that this space is functional for what you choose to do with it. No one can tell you what to do in your personal space, because it is yours!

HYGGE MUSIC AND MOVIES

Another great way to keep hygge in your heart at all times is to choose music and movies that give you comfort and joy. Pick music and movies you can enjoy with your loved ones, and if you have kids, choose kid-friendly media as well. Try to select options that can brighten your spirits and help you feel light and free.

For example, stay away from music with violent or upsetting lyrics, and pick soothing, softer songs instead. But don't forget to listen to your favorite bands and singers now and then, too. Even if you love loud rock music, this music can be hygge if you listen to it for the purpose of enjoyment and calming down your busy life for a little while.

While it's better to avoid music with troubling lyrics most of the time, you can listen to it when you're in the right frame of mind. Just don't let this type of music get in the way of your hygge experience, and don't let your children listen to this type of music with you until they are old enough to not let it interfere with their hygge, either.

The same goes for movies. This suggestion doesn't mean that you can never watch movies with heavy themes or upsetting content. Sometimes, these movies can help you learn to better process your own feelings and thoughts within the safe space of a fictional story. In other words, movies like this can sometimes be cathartic. However, it's important to approach this type of movie with the right frame of mind. Don't watch an upsetting or violent movie when you're already feeling emotionally low or unhappy about something. If you have children, don't view these kinds of movies around them, either.

Music and movies don't have to be all happy all the time, and you don't have to surround yourself only with spa-like sounds or documentary-style films to benefit from your entertainment. Just remember, as with everything else, approach the media you enjoy with a hygge mind and never choose movies or music that prevent you from feeling comfortable or cozy.

HYGGE SELF-CARE

There are many ways you can practice hygge self-care. They may be as simple as buying a small, low-cost gift or treat for yourself, or as elaborate as an at-home spa day. Take care of yourself in whichever ways bring you a sense of calm and happiness. Don't overdo it with money, or you may stress about your budget. And don't take so much time for self-care that you forget to spend time with your friends and family, either.

Start small by sprucing up your personal space or setting aside an hour for a bubble bath and some relaxation time. From there, you can look for other methods of self-care you may want to try. Here are a few types of self-care you can practice, ranging from the easy and affordable to the more elaborate:

- Buy a nice bath bomb and take a long, relaxing bath. **Pick one that won't stain your tub, so you don't have to worry about scrubbing it right after you finish your relaxation time.**

- Make yourself a favorite cup of tea and sit under a blanket while you drink it. **Put on some of your favorite music quietly in the background as you sip.**

- Check out a book from the library on a subject of interest. **Take a half hour every day to read it and expand your horizons a little more.**

- Touch something with a texture you enjoy, such as a soft pillow or even a plush toy. **You may also want to try buying a stress relief ball for yourself, so you can have a positive tactile experience during your relax time.**

- Rearrange your personal space a little. **You don't have to spend any money to do this, but just use your existing items instead. Move things around so that they're a little more efficient and organized for your hygge experience.**

- Treat yourself to a new shirt, pair of pants, or whole outfit. **Don't overdo it when it comes to the price tag, but pick something that complements your style and makes you feel good to wear it.**

- Treat yourself to a massage or a spa day, but only if you have the time and money to do so. This indulgence is not a requirement to practice hygge self-care, and should only be considered a bonus, so don't overspend!

CHAPTER 4:

HYGGE AT WORK

Hygge may seem like it has nothing to do with business or work. After all, the very idea of work is often not relaxing or cozy. Instead, work calls to mind the image of agonizingly long days and lots of stress, which is a common work environment for most Americans and Europeans. Longer work hours make a healthy work-life balance difficult to achieve, which is a problem, especially in American culture. Working hard is considered an admirable quality in American workers, often to the point where workers can experience illness from stress and lack of breaks. Family leave is disappearing, and many employees feel pressured to not take any of their vacation time. Many workers do not have any paid sick leave and cannot take off from work when they fall ill, either.

It does not have to be this way, though. You may not be able to control every aspect of your job or career, but you can start making small changes here and there to ease the burden, especially if you're looking to head in the direction of freedom via self-employment. Make your workplace as hygge as possible to reduce stress and displeasure.

Adjust your attitude about work. Work is not life. You work to live; you should not live to work. Work is not the sole priority, so set limits on how much you work and when work can contact you. This mindset is not always possible in some fields. If you are on call, try to make the best of your free time to do hobbies or be with your family. Conserve your time as best you can in your line of work.

Not everyone can do what they love, but if you can, then do it without fear or doubt. Maybe it is finally time that you open your dream restaurant or quit your job to try traveling the world and make money blogging. Sometimes you may need to sacrifice money for happiness. Adjust your attitude to value happiness over money, and take a pay cut to do what you love if possible. When you die, the amount of money you made will not matter to you — how happy you were will.

Evaluate your budget to determine what you can relinquish and how much money you can safely lose if you need to change your career. Take some vacation time when you can afford it. Consider reducing your hours, or even explore new job options in a field that you enjoy. It is more important to have a life you enjoy than many expensive material possessions. Hygge encourages you to value moments and experiences over meaningless possessions and money. Just make sure you are able to make ends meet where necessary (such as rent, electricity, and groceries) and proceed from there.

Some people, such as artists, are lucky enough to do what they love. The only problem is that it is easy for these people to forget about other important elements of life as they become addicted to their jobs. If you are such a person, remember that there is more to life than your job. As exciting as your job is, you need to do other things you love, including spending time with your family or exercising outside. Never devote everything you have to your job, because your job is only a fraction of what your life is about.

MAKE YOUR WORKPLACE SURROUNDINGS MORE HYGGE

By now, you know very well that the décor and colors used in a room can greatly affect the mood and productivity of a person. Danish offices look different than those in other countries because the Danish understand the work environment can influence how you work and how you feel about the work.

Whether you are working at a desk, in an office, or at home, make sure your workspace is clean and uncluttered. Being organized can stop the day from being too hectic and can make you feel better all around. Imagine how much time you will save if you are not busy looking for things in a huge mess. And think of how much better you will feel if you walk into a clear space where you can breathe and not worry about stepping on something or having something fall on you.

If you have any choice in the décor and color around you, choose light colors or white with a pattern. This ideal décor is not distracting and will not negatively affect mood or performance. You don't need tons of pictures or distracting knick-knacks on your walls or desk. However, you can really enhance your mood at work by having a few things that bring you joy, such as a nice note from a boss or customer, or a cute photo of your kids.

Some people benefit from a vision board, where they attach pictures of their goals and cherished ideals. You can use a vision board to help you visualize your goals and feel inspired to achieve those goals. Use it as a means for productivity and mood enhancement, but don't get bogged down feeling negatively toward yourself if it takes you some time to achieve your goals.

Use a comforting scent. If you have a stressful job, try a lavender diffuser to bring relaxation into your atmosphere. If you need energy, try scents like citrus or rosemary. If you need comfort in an emotionally challenging job, find a scent that reminds you of good times, and use an essential oil or scented candle to bring into your workspace. For just a few bucks, you can get a wax warmer that will diffuse scent throughout your workspace.

Comfort is key. You can't expect to work well if your environment is unpleasant and uncomfortable. Ergonomic keypads, mice, chairs, and desks can add so much comfort to your workplace. You can also use a cushion or neck pillow to make your chair more comfortable. If you can't decorate your workspace as you please, then just add little things, like a colorful tissue box or a jar of candy. Be sure to wear comfortable shoes and clothes. Even in a formal setting, you don't have to wear business clothes that make you want to faint. If you walk during your commute to work, you can wear comfortable shoes such as tennis shoes or sandals and just carry your work shoes in your bag to change into at the office. Make sure your clothes match the current weather, so that you can maintain good body temperature. Don't wear anything so tight that it digs into your skin as you work. If you have to wear a uniform, make sure it fits and loosen it by undoing a button or taking off your belt or tie during your downtime.

ATTITUDE

The way you perceive situations can greatly change how you feel about them, and sometimes it can even change the outcome. Hygge at work is all about your attitude and the way you carry yourself.

First of all, remove the urgency. Even if you have an urgent deadline, or if you are in the business of saving lives, you can reduce stress by removing the idea that your job is life or death. Your job very well may be life or death, but don't focus on that. Instead, focus on the tasks at hand. Don't think, "I have to do this by midnight, or it is over for me!" Think, "I have 'this many' steps to complete before I reach my deadline at midnight. So, this is how I will divvy up the tasks over the remaining hours." Approach things from a problem-solving angle. Don't focus on what might happen if you fail, or what you stand to lose. This attitude reduces your stress and makes work more pleasurable. When your mind wanders, use mindfulness to bring it back into focus.

Confidence is also key to reducing your stress and improving your mood. You don't feel that great when you are busy criticizing yourself or feeling inadequate, do you? Believe in yourself. Let yourself take calculated risks that will grow your business or your team's performance. Try innovative things. If you fail, learn from that experience instead of beating yourself up over it. When you are confident in your abilities, you can look beyond yourself and seek out others who are good at what they do.

Another excellent method of improving your attitude at work is to work on your cooperation skills. Cooperation is what makes businesses run well. When you are confident, you aren't egotistical and jealous of others. Rather, you are open to appreciating and working with others. You put away your ego and become open to others. That's a great way to be at work! Work will be easier when you strive to work with others and make valuable connections, without letting jealousy and ego get in the way. Your confidence will also make you more attractive to others, so they will want to talk to you and work with you.

Connect with your co-workers and have fun with them. **Work hard to collaborate with others.** If you prefer to work alone, at least make water cooler chitchat to connect with others in your workplace. The day will go by faster, and you will rest easier knowing that you have co-workers who will help you out when you need it.

Finally, keep the attitude that your work is only one part of your life. **Place value on other things, like hobbies and family.**

51

WORK-LIFE BALANCE

Hygge encourages you to live your life moment by moment. It encourages you to be with your family and friends. That can be difficult when you are stuck at work all the time, but you must strike a balance between work and the rest of your life. Devote some time to work, but use good time management to get everything done. Then set boundaries and don't work when you don't have to. Take some time for yourself and your loved ones where work may not intrude.

Work-life balance requires you to find time for things other than work. This means that you should not feel guilty or afraid of taking a vacation. It also means that you don't answer work emails when you are at home with your family, and when you are out to dinner, you don't answer work-related phone calls unless absolutely necessary. Have automatic vacation responses set up on your email that inform people when you will get back to them. As tempting as it is to respond right then and there, get back to them when you say you will, not during your time off. Most people are accepting and understanding when you set these boundaries. Without these boundaries, your workaholic nature will become the standard that people expect from you.

If your job does not allow you to have an adequate work-life balance, then consider switching jobs or even careers. It may take some time to move into a new position, but you should work for it. You need a job that does not treat you like a machine.

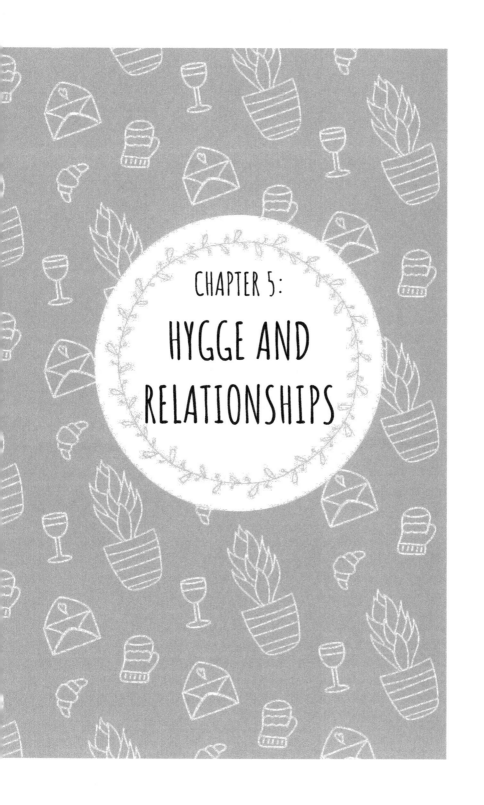

CHAPTER 5:

HYGGE AND RELATIONSHIPS

Wouldn't it be nice if stress and drama could be removed from your relationships? It may seem impossible to think that simply changing your lifestyle a little could make you happier in all your relationships. People spend years in therapy to try and get it right, and sometimes still fail. Hygge cannot guarantee compatibility, but it can help you to find peace in your dealings with your spouses, parents, colleagues, and children, if everyone can compromise and make a few adjustments.

FINANCIAL SECURITY

How many fights have you had involving money? Danish marriages, excluding the royal family perhaps, are much different from many other marriages around the world.

Firstly, the average age of both men and women getting married is above 30. This later age means that many individuals are already financially settled before they bring another person into the mix. No matter what age you are when you get married, strive to be financially sound before you make that commitment. If you are already married, then take some time to focus on outlining and achieving your financial goals. You should work hard together to remove any financial strife that causes problems in your marriage.

Many Danish people also do not have the kind of lavish weddings that so many other women feel pressured to host. Many Western women often seek to outdo every other woman with their weddings, and a high price tag often means years of credit card debt. Yet this competitive approach may not be the best way to start out a new family, even if the wedding is a beautiful moment. The wedding should be about the couple, not pleasing and impressing everyone else. A simpler wedding is sometimes better. Consider minimizing stress and focusing on enjoying your partner instead of having an enormous, fancy wedding.

Throughout marriage, sound decisions are made by many Danish couples to ensure savings and living only within their means. Eliminating fights over bills can bring you and your partner much closer together. Create a budget together and stick to it. If you don't need something or can't afford it, then don't buy it. Focus on enjoying the little moments together than squandering money on what you don't really need.

NO DRAMA

Drama has become a part of American culture, and everyone seems to find a way to create it or place themselves inside of it, whether intentionally or not. Then they wonder why divorce rates are so high and why they are so unhappy. Drama has no place in a healthy relationship, so picking your battles is critical. Being right isn't always going to feel good when it means going to bed alone.

Of course you will fight, but try to fight fair. Don't reduce it to name-calling and dredging up past wrongs. Fight with a purpose, and do not go to bed angry. Try to reach a resolution rather than hurting each other. You have heard it a million times, but fighting fair really is key, and that applies for all relationships, not just romantic ones.

CREATING ROMANTIC MOMENTS

In a romantic relationship, you want to create memorable moments. These romantic moments don't entail expensive dinners at fancy five-star restaurants or island vacations that break the bank. They don't involve presents of diamonds or hundred-dollar rose bouquets. Sure, those ideas are romantic, and you can practice them with your partner whenever you are able, but you can create romance even when you are broke or tired after work. All you have to do is be thoughtful and think of what your partner may want.

Offer your partner a foot rub or a bubble bath after a long day at work. Surprise them with their favorite dinner. Suggest an evening walk. Pick some flowers and present your partner with a handmade bouquet. Or try the Danish practice of taking long walks together out in nature. These little actions show that you care. When you make an effort, your partner will notice and reciprocate, and your relationship will grow stronger and better.

Also, strive for more frequent deep conversations with your partner. Conversation bonds you and your partner. It helps you get to know each other. Your partner will feel more loved and appreciated if you take some time to talk to him or her. Simply taking the time to ask about his or her day and thanking your partner for being in your life can make a world of difference. Some married couples careening toward divorce have been able to save their marriages merely by saying thank you more often and asking each other about their days.

HYGGE AND FRIENDSHIPS

Of course, your relationships are not limited to romantic involvement. You most likely have several friends and acquaintances. Your relationship with your romantic partner is not the same as your relationship with your friends, of course, but you can still practice hygge throughout your friendships. There are many different ways to keep hygge in your heart when interacting with your friends. Here are a few tips you can keep in mind to maintain hygge in your friendships:

- Take time while getting to know a new person. **When you meet someone new, you may be tempted to jump right into being close with him or her— or, on the other hand, you may not think you'd be compatible as friends. Either way, don't let your first impressions cloud your relationships with new people. Work slowly through the first stages of any relationship. This pace can make it easier for you to connect with others and to find ways to bond with them, and it can also help you determine those people whom you may not want to get to know more closely, too.**

- Set aside time to spend with your friends each week. **Lives can get busy even when you are trying your best to practice hygge, and it may not always be possible to meet up with your friends in person every week. However, make sure you're at least connecting with them weekly to see what's going on in their lives. You may have to achieve this contact through texting or phone calls, especially if your friends don't live close enough for you to drop by their houses. These types of conversations can be just as enriching when you devote your full attention to your friends and make them a part of your regular hygge routine.**

- Go out of your way to remember a few details about your friends. You don't have to remember everything they tell you—and they don't have to do that for you, either. But if you go out of your way to try to remember a few specifics, your friends will be happy and you'll have the joy and comfort of knowing you contributed to their happiness, too. This concept goes beyond just remembering their birthdays, and it also includes keeping track of details, like their favorite color or something they may collect. Keeping this knowledge handy can also make it easier for you to choose gifts for your friends when necessary, too!

- Spend time in person with your friends whenever possible. Of course, it's not always possible for your schedule to work out with your friends' calendars, and it may not be easy to spend time together in-person frequently. Try to reach out and offer to do things with your friends in person when you can. If your friends reach out to you, try not to turn them down every time, or they may stop asking after a while. Keeping up with a friendship can be challenging, but it can also be very rewarding. Making time for your friends is a very hygge concept and can help you feel more comfortable and happier, too.

- Don't be afraid to invite friends along for big family outings. Yes, your friends may have their own families, but they may also want to join yours for some experiences and events, too. If you and your friend both have families, why not try inviting them all along for a big group get-together? Try having a cookout in the backyard with both families involved. This way, you can spend time with all of the people who matter the most in your life, and your friend can do the same thing. You can practice hygge in this way by setting aside time to spend with people who bring you joy and comfort.

- If you fight with your friend, try to remain calm when working it out. Everyone fights sometimes; that's human nature. However, when you are trying to keep things hygge in your life, it's important to work through disagreements and problems as quickly and easily as possible. You do not have to apologize for everything when a fight happens, because fights are a two-way street. Be sure you apologize genuinely for the parts of the fight that you may have contributed to. Stay calm when you do this and don't say things to guilt or aggravate your friend further. It can be hard to learn how to recover from a fight while keeping things hygge, but it is possible to do so.

- When giving gifts to your friends, keep them simple and comfortable to stick with the hygge theme. Don't give your friends anything that is too expensive for you to fit into your budget, and don't give them presents that are too large for their homes, or that might disturb their hygge decor. Try to choose presents that are meaningful, functional, or both when gift-giving the hygge way. You may also want to try making homemade presents, which can help you incorporate your hygge hobbies into your friendships too.

Whether you are just getting to know a new friend or you're interacting with someone you've known most of your life, you can keep these ideas in mind when spending time with your friends. Hygge doesn't have to stop with your romantic relationships. Best of all, if you practice hygge in your friendships, you may be able to convince your friends to join in the hygge experience, too! In this way, you'll be spreading the spirit of coziness and comfort to everyone you know.

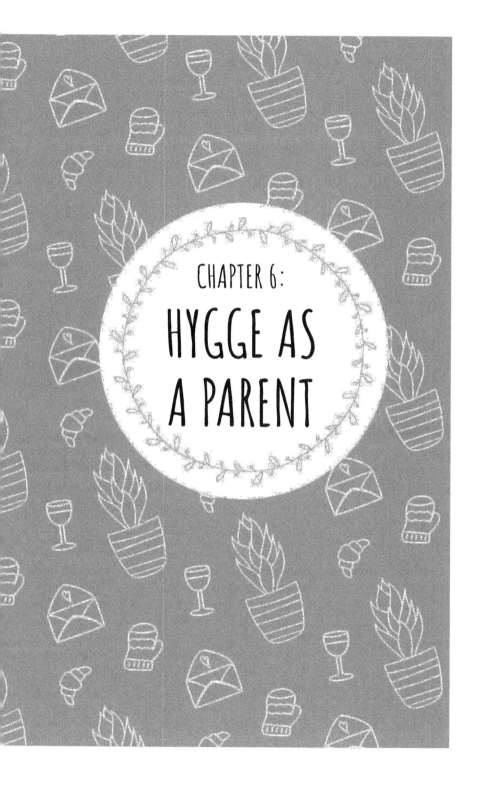

CHAPTER 6:

HYGGE AS A PARENT

The parent-child relationship is often overlooked when it comes to improving the way you feel with other people, but it is one of the most important relationships you will ever have. Your relationship with your children sets up a model for their future relationships. It is important to cultivate love, trust, and independence. Hygge can be a huge help in achieving this proactive parenting goal. Plus, trying some Danish parenting tips may give you relief if you are struggling with how things are going with your children currently. Here are some hygge tips on parenting that might help transform a chaotic home into a more loving and comfortable one:

- Redirecting represents the first line of discipline instead of going straight to spanking or time outs to modify the child's behavior, especially later in life. Many acts of misbehavior resonate from emotions that a child just does not know how to express yet. Redirect the child on how to express themselves properly, and the behavior will change. Ask them, "What are you feeling right now? Is there another way you can show what you are feeling instead of [insert bad behavior]?"

- Playing is growing. There is a reason the Montessori method is popular in schools: Play is considered an essential part of learning and development for children. Play with them often and let them use their imagination. This approach will foster excellent critical and creative thinking skills in young adulthood.

- Have children help with chores as soon as they are physically able. Not only will chores get done quicker, meaning more time for fun together, but children will also feel more self-worth in knowing that they can help an adult with something.

- Have uninterrupted time together where everyone enjoys doing things as a family. Turn off electronics and be with your kids wholeheartedly. Have meaningful conversations with them and get to know them as individuals, as challenging as it may be to consider them anything but your babies. Let them express themselves. Make sure there is something in it for everyone. Ensure that no one is excluded, and all of you are in the moment with each other.

HYGGE FAMILY MOMENTS

It is easy to create family moments that you can cherish for years to come. Even the smallest activities can become wonderful memories. From fishing trips to day excursions to local museums, use the resources available to create little moments together. You don't have to spend a lot of money to enjoy family moments.

Most people today have busy schedules, and they hardly have time to sit down and eat. Make a conscious effort to get all family members at the dinner table every evening. Talk about each other's days. This unity will create a bond with your family, making you closer as a unit. If you have a family member who absolutely cannot eat with you because of work or school, coordinate your schedules and set aside a few hours to spend time together. Just trying to spend time together will mean a lot to your family and encourage them to make time for you.

If you're looking for a hygge-appropriate family vacation, try going on a camping trip together. This suggestion may seem a little old-fashioned, and depending on how attached your kids are to their phones and electronics, it may take some work to get them to agree to go. A well-planned family camping trip can go a long way toward improving your whole household's hygge experience, as well as helping you bond with your kids and partner.

A camping trip doesn't have to be a long one to make a positive impact. Even if you just take a weekend getaway trip to the local campsite, you and your family can have a great time with each other. Don't worry about spending a ton of money on expensive camping gear or renting a cabin or RV for the trip. Just take a tent and the essentials along, and plan to cook everything you eat on-site, too. This way, you won't be spending so much that you feel stressed by the costs, and you won't have your comfortable family experience interrupted by worries about money.

It may be a little difficult to be physically comfortable when camping, but that doesn't mean you can't be emotionally cozy the whole time. Bring along battery-powered lights and set up a cozy atmosphere after the sun goes down. If anyone in your family plays an instrument, encourage them to take it along and have a group sing-along together. Keep coziness in mind at all times when you're camping together with your loved ones and you will likely have a beautiful hygge experience that will provide memories to last a lifetime.

If you don't live anywhere close to nature, you could consider planning a staycation in your city instead. Stay in an affordable hotel or even try a hostel. Visit local museums and other nearby attractions that are affordable and easy to get to.

CHAPTER 7:
HYGGE IN THE SEASON AND HOLIDAYS

WINTER HOLIDAYS

Christmas, Hanukkah, and Kwanzaa are some of the most hygge holidays because they are naturally cozy. Invite the winter holidays into your home by preparing ahead of time. Focus more on having family gatherings with hot cocoa, singing carols, sharing stories, and making cookies together, rather than on buying the most expensive presents for each other and decorating your house more lavishly than your neighbors' homes. And don't forget that Danish Christmas tradition of giving special treats to the animals in your life, too! Remember what these holidays are about: love, cheer, family, and coziness.

Winter holiday decorations can help you keep the hygge spirit going all winter long. Don't choose noisy, bright, flashing decorations or multicolored lights. Instead, pick more muted colors and gentle themes like snowflakes, silver and gold colors, and winter forests. Choose one or two colors for your lights instead of all sorts of different colors at once. And don't decorate with items that play loud sounds or music.

Another important concept to keep in mind when practicing hygge during the winter holidays is to let your family or friends be involved with your plans whenever possible. Are you going shopping for gifts for your kids? Bring along a friend! Are you going to a friend's holiday party? Ask if it's okay to bring your romantic partner along, too. There are many ways to make sure you're spending time with the people you love during the holiday season. This togetherness can help you keep things hygge during this cozy time of the year.

You may want to invite your kids to help you decorate during the holidays, too. This collaboration can be a fun way to create family bonding experiences that will encourage your children to remain positive and upbeat during the season, too. After you decorate together, take time to settle down with some hot cocoa and a kid-friendly holiday movie.

Remember, too, that it's easy to get bogged down with the stress of the holidays. During this time of year, you're likely to encounter chaos everywhere you turn, whether it's in the form of a noisy ad or a busy shopping center. There are plenty of opportunities to get overwhelmed, frustrated, and upset when this time of year approaches, but remember that this is not good hygge. It's always essential to set aside time for yourself so you can remain calm during the holidays. This act of self-care can help you clear your mind and remain mindful enough to form lasting memories.

Remember, as with anything, hygge is not about overindulgence or stress. If you're going to be cooking often during the winter holidays, cook only what you need and try not to be wasteful. When serving your family for the holidays, don't spend a fortune on expensive ingredients when more affordable ones will work just as well—or even better. The same holds true of giving gifts during the holiday season.

Maybe you have some traveling to do during the winter to visit your family in other parts of the country. Depending on where you live, this may be a daunting task. You might have to fly or drive a very long way to get there. Although it's always important to see your friends and family when you can, especially around the holidays, try not to stress too much about this type of travel if possible. Do everything you can ahead of time to make the trip as easy as you can.

If you're going to be traveling by air, start planning far enough in advance that you aren't scrambling at the last minute and buying expensive plane tickets just a few days before your trip. Do your research and determine what you'll be allowed to bring on the plane and what you may need to check or leave behind. If you're traveling with kids or pets, learn those rules and regulations too.

If you'll be driving for a long distance, plan your route as well as some backup routes ahead of time. If you need to stay overnight on your drive to visit family, reserve your hotel rooms far enough in advance that you won't have to pay last-minute prices for them. This precaution can help you reduce the stress levels you may experience during your trip as well.

THANKSGIVING

Thanksgiving is another very important family-oriented holiday that can help you improve your hygge experience. Plan to have a big meal with your family, but remember that there's no need to overdo it. Just because a large turkey with several side dishes and desserts may be what you see on TV versions of the holiday doesn't mean you have to stress yourself out cooking so much for your family. Make enough food that everyone can get full and enjoy themselves, but tone it down whenever possible, too.

This is another holiday you can celebrate while getting your kids involved. Invite your children to learn a little bit about cooking by helping out in the kitchen. Even if your kids are very little, they can stir or decorate food (as long as you don't mind having to clean up afterward!). This way, the whole family can bond together over cooking a meal. You may even want to try putting together a meal that is full of hygge ingredients, which you can find in our section on hygge cooking later on in this book.

Thanksgiving, like Christmas, is a holiday that is about togetherness. There's nothing more hygge than spending time with the people you love and being mindful of that time so you can truly enjoy it and remember it later on. Be sure to remain mindful in everything you do throughout the Thanksgiving holiday.

Keep in mind, too, that traditions can be a nice way to practice hygge, but they aren't required. Maybe you have a tradition of making Thanksgiving dessert with your child, but now your child has gone away to college. Instead of being caught up in the negative feelings surrounding this change and allowing them to impact your hygge experience in a bad way, try to consider the way your relationship has bloomed and grown. The good feelings associated with those memories were not about making the dessert, but about spending time with your child. For this reason, you can approach this in a hygge way and make new memories by being positive and mindful of the time you spend with your child, even if you don't bake together anymore.

Don't forget to decorate for Thanksgiving with hygge in mind. This is a holiday that focuses on warm, soft colors, so use those comfortable shades of brown, tan, and yellow whenever possible in your dinner decor. Light candles and keep the lights low during your Thanksgiving dinner for a great hygge experience, too.

NEW YEAR'S

Even the New Year can be hygge with a little practice. New Year's Eve is typically a celebration that's all about making noise and partying hard. Even if you want to let loose, drink, and be merry, there's no reason you can't keep hygge in your heart at the same time. Spend this holiday with your friends and family, and don't forget to take this time to express gratitude to them for being a part of your life. When you count down to the start of the new year, practice being mindful of the experience and truly living it. Don't look at your phone or computer through the whole event!

You can also make hygge your New Year's resolution. If you're not practicing hygge yet, or if you feel like you could do better with it, make it your resolution and set hygge goals for yourself throughout the year. Just remember not to stress yourself out in learning to practice hygge. This is a process, so don't worry if you aren't getting it right immediately. Any New Year's resolution is meant to be worked on throughout the year, rather than changed abruptly.

BIRTHDAYS

What about celebrating birthdays? Can they be hygge as well? Absolutely! If you are an adult, your birthday may seem like a negative experience. You may find yourself wishing you weren't getting older, but remember that time doesn't stop for anyone, and aging is a normal and acceptable part of your life. Try not to let yourself feel too stressed out about getting older; instead, be mindful and live in the moment whenever possible. We are not promised even one more day, so be thankful and appreciative that you've been given another year to work on improving your life and experiences.

If you have children, they may be a lot more excited about their birthdays than you are about yours. Don't let your negativity about your own birthday interfere with your children's happiness about theirs—and try to integrate some of that happiness into your own birthday experiences, too. When you have kids, it's important to set aside a special time to celebrate their birthdays. Make this time all about your children and help them understand that it's a time to be happy and excited, more than just getting presents.

Sometimes, it's not possible to celebrate a birthday on the actual date. Adults usually understand this, but kids may have trouble with this concept. If this delay happens within your family, make sure you set aside time to celebrate the birthday in question even if it can't be on the right date. This approach can help your child (or even you) feel a little more special.

Decorate for birthdays in a hygge way. You don't need to go all out with an expensive cake, and you can even try baking your own cake with the help of your family for a more hygge experience.

Finally, no matter who in your life is having a birthday, be sure you give gifts that are thoughtful and meaningful in some way, or functional. If possible, try to do all three! Of course, most kids want to get toys and electronics for their birthdays, and you can give these kinds of presents too as long as you don't overdo it. Remember not to give items that are going to cost so much you end up stressing about money instead of enjoying your loved one's special day. Don't offer presents that are just going to become clutter and make life disorganized for the person you're gifting.

OTHER HOLIDAYS

While the winter holidays are possibly the most hygge, you can make every holiday hygge by really getting into the spirit. Go all out with candy for trick-or-treaters and have fun on Halloween, give your kids candy on Easter, and go to local events and spend time with family and friends for any holiday at any time of the year. These suggestions entail embracing the holidays and enjoying the moment, which signify hygge in a nutshell.

Some people feel disgruntled or annoyed when the holidays roll around. Why not enjoy yourself? The holidays don't have to be stressful or commercial, just because the media and others around you make them so. Rather, the holidays are an excuse to take a break from work, enjoy yourself, and enjoy good food. Forget about your diet. Forget about being the best. Let go of work concerns. Just allow the holiday spirit overtake you and make it a special time for yourself and your loved ones!

SPRING

Spring is a fun time when the earth begins to wake up from winter. The cold lingers, but the days are pleasant. Take advantage of the energy of spring by doing some spring cleaning and airing out your house. Go outside and show your kids the magic of nature by pointing out bird nests and budding flowers.

Although this time of the year is excellent to enjoy nature with your family, it's also still a little cool outside. It's still a good time of the year to curl up with a hot cup of tea under a soft blanket, especially in the evenings! Another nice way to practice hygge during the springtime is to sip your morning cup of coffee slowly while you admire the sunrise. You might have to get up a little earlier than usual to do so, but it can help you start your day off with a comfortable frame of mind that can keep you calm and organized throughout the rest of the day.

Spring is always a viable time to do a little spring cleaning and reorganizing, too. If you're looking for a way to improve your hygge at home, try setting aside a few days for you and your whole family to get involved with cleaning. Organize your closets and get rid of anything you may not have worn or used over the past year. Spring cleaning is not a requirement for hygge, but it is a great way to bring many of the aspects of hygge into your home during this refreshing time of the year.

Don't forget to stop and think about the way nature is changing around you as spring dawns. This time of year represents birth, fresh starts, and life. Bringing these concepts into your daily routine can help you feel more at peace and mindful of the world around you.

SUMMER

Summer is a fun time when you can enjoy yourself outside. Make the most of summer by getting in touch with nature. Plan a lot of outdoor excursions and hikes. Plant a garden and grow some of your own fruits and vegetables. If you have kids, they will love the experience of growing food, too. Take advantage of the precious summer months and the fact that school is out to spend time with your family. Embrace the short time that summer allows for outdoor barbecues, firecrackers, and sports like volleyball, swimming, or softball.

If you live in a very hot climate, it may be difficult to go outside often during this time of the year. If this is the case, try to get out in the morning before the temperature climbs too high, or make plans to go out after dark or to enjoy some sunsets. Just because it's very hot outside, that doesn't mean you can't spend time enjoying nature with the people you love. It just requires you to think a little differently about the types of outdoor activities you may want to enjoy during these months.

School may be on break for your kids, but work doesn't usually stop for adults during the summertime. It can be difficult to go to work with a positive mindset when it's hot and you just want to go on vacation. Just remember to keep up with your hygge at work, and double your efforts during summer when you may need it most.

If you're taking a summer vacation with your family, don't stress too much about planning it. Try not to spend too much money or cause yourself any additional worry about finances by taking an elaborate trip. While a big, expensive cruise or a trip overseas may sound like fun, your budget might not allow it. You can have just as much fun staying closer to home and enjoying the relaxation and comforts of a hygge vacation with your family. You may even discover some local places of interest you've never heard of before!

AUTUMN

Autumn is a cooling down time, when you can enjoy the transition from summer to winter. Use this period to prepare your house for the coming winter by filling it with candles and warm blankets. Make warm soups and teas. Harvest your garden and enjoy the fruits of your labor. If you have a lot of trees in your yard, rake the leaves and proceed to play in the piles with your pet or your kids, or even your romantic partner, for some silly fun. Go for hikes in the brisk autumn air and observe the migrating birds. These activities allow you to embrace the essence of fall.

Nature isn't the only way you can enjoy fall and bring hygge into your life at the same time. This is a wonderful time of year for wearing some of your most comfortable clothing, so don't forget to bring out those light, soft sweaters and other cozy clothes that embody the hygge spirit. Most clothes and decorations at this time of the year are available in warm, earthy colors that enhance the feeling of hygge when you see them. Stick to these autumn shades whenever possible, even when choosing the candles and blankets you'll use in your home as the weather turns cooler.

When it's brisk at night but not too cold, this is an excellent time of year to go out and stargaze. The cooler air and fewer clouds make it easier to see the night sky, and it's comfortable enough to sit outside in the evening without having to worry as much about insects as you do during the summer. If you have time and are able to do so, drive away from the city lights and explore nature to stargaze with your family. You can also take this opportunity to learn and teach your children about the stars you can see from your region or even from your own backyard.

During the fall, prepare to decorate for and celebrate Halloween and Thanksgiving with your family. Have fun with this, but do so mindfully and without being overwhelmed by too many requirements you may set for yourself as the holiday season approaches

WINTER

Danish winters are cold and dark and seem to last forever. Do the Danes let the winter get them down? No, they make the best of winters by inviting warmth, coziness, and cheer into their homes. Don't allow snow and darkness to upset you; rather, make a game of playing in the snow and use winter as an excuse to make a lot of warm, delicious food. Bring out your comfy sweaters, sweatpants and slippers. While shoveling snow and salting the driveway, sing songs to keep you warm and have your kids help. It may be challenging to keep your spirits high during the coldest times of the year, but it is possible with the right hygge mindset

Winter is the best time of year to practice making some of your favorite comfort foods. If you're not used to cooking, you may want to start with something easy like chicken noodle soup or homemade bread. You can also try making brownies, cookies, and other fun treats for your family. If you're a little more experienced in the kitchen, why not branch out with recipes you've never tried before that include comforting ingredients? You might even want to make something completely unique for your next big holiday meal. Don't forget to get the kids involved, or invite your partner or friends to join you for a cooking activity.

CHAPTER 8:
FOOD AND DRINKS

Did you know that the concept of hygge comes with its own diet? Well, it's not exactly a diet. It is not guaranteed to help you lose weight. It is not even something that should be in used with every single meal. But keeping hygge in mind when you're cooking and eating can help you get the full effect of this lifestyle. With an emphasis on comfort food, great smells, and warmth, how could you not want to give it a try?

SCANDI COMFORT FOODS

If you never had Scandinavian comfort food, you are truly missing some wonderful cuisines. There is something special about every aspect of this food, and there is nothing that says hygge more than sitting down to slowly enjoy a delicious, homemade meal with friends and family. That is truly the point of this idea: to eat in comfort. There is no rush. There is a steady conversation throughout the meal that you savor, just as a meal is meant to be. Can you incorporate a meal like this once a week? If you would like to try, there are many hygge recipe books available, as the concept is gaining popularity around the world and in many cultures. In a hygge cookbook, you might find comfort food recipes involving ingredients such as:

• Duck

• Potatoes

• Rye Bread

• Quinoa Salad

• Apples

WARM DRINKS

Hygge drinks are traditionally meant for those cold winter nights spent curled up in front of a fire. The aromas are soothing, making you think of your childhood, the holidays, and pure warmth, and so is the temperature of the drink itself. It shouldn't be hard to think of something warm you like to drink, but just in case, here are some of the best hygge suggestions:

• Apple Cider

• Coffee

• Herbal or Green Tea

• Hot Chocolate

A HYGGE RECIPE FOR EVERY MEAL

If you have never cooked any Scandinavian comfort food before, or anything even close, you might be wondering what to try. Baking is a huge part of the Scandinavian cuisine, but you can't live exclusively on bread and cookies, as much as you might like to. So, we have prepared a suggestion for each meal to get you started. In sum, we offer three days of choices to try a new comforting meal with your whole family. The best part is that many of the recipes for hygge meals can be prepared together as a family, allowing you to spend even more time with your loved ones. This time together is a precious commodity, if work and school always seem to get in the way of quality time.

For breakfast, try an apple turnover or similar pastry. Many Europeans have their sweet treats in the morning to get a boost for the day. This tradition has been working for them for many years. Why not try your hand at it and see how you feel?

For lunch, nothing says "hygge" better than a warm and hearty soup. There are many varieties to choose from that are all delicious. However, pumpkin soup is by far the general favorite. You can dress it up any way you want and drink it right from a large mug.

For dinner, why not try something savory? Roasted pork is a common staple at the Danish dinner table. Pair it with a baked potato for an indulgent meal that does not involve anything fried or pre-made. This is the exact kind of meal you can savor at the table with your loved ones.

There are many places you can find hygge recipes online. Here are three sites to get you started with hygge cooking:

- http://www.organicauthority.com/discovering-danish-food-with-9-recipes-to-make-you-feel-the-hygge/

- http://www.self.com/gallery/13-healthy-hygge-foods-for-the-coziest-day-ever

- https://www.brit.co/hygge-foods-recipes/

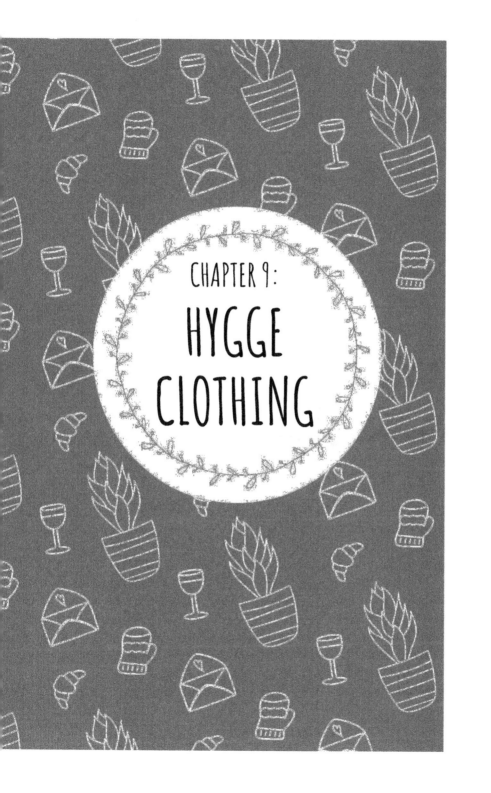

CHAPTER 9:
HYGGE CLOTHING

Hygge does not place strong emphasis on external appearances. Rather, it focuses on how you feel. It is better to be lounging on the couch in sweats enjoying yourself than looking like a beauty king or queen. While looking fashionable has its benefits, it is not the most important goal in the hygge lifestyle. You will enjoy life more if you relax.

Danish clothes are often simple and functional. They don't look bad, but they don't sacrifice quality for appearance. Wearing simple, clean, quality clothes is essential to your comfort. Clothes with pockets are useful for carrying things. You want to select clothes that don't restrict your body or make you hold a ridiculous posture all day long.

Go for a good fit, not a tight fit. Also, go for materials that feel good to you. Cotton is light and breathable during summer. Warm wool and wool blends are nice during winter. You can get the most out of sweat-wicking polyester when you are engaged in strenuous tasks or sports.

Shoes should also be comfortable. Why wear skyscraper heels when you have to walk, or tight shoes that hurt your toes and give you blisters? Instead, wear practical shoes that fit you well. Sometimes you must sacrifice beauty for comfort—otherwise, your day could often be disrupted by your aching feet. An oozing blister is not worth the compliments you'll receive. It's better to buy shoes that fit so that you are able to walk around with ease.

HYGGE SPRING CLOTHES

Spring clothes are some of the most comfortable out there. These clothes are often made of soft fabrics that allow your skin to breathe while still keeping you warm enough on cooler spring nights. They are usually available in pastels as well as soft, muted earth tones, which are all excellent color choices for a hygge wardrobe. Don't forget to bring a jacket along when you go outside during the spring, especially in the earlier part of the year. Pick clothes that give you lots of room to move around comfortably while remaining warm enough for this season.

HYGGE SUMMER CLOTHES

Stay comfortable when it's hot outside by focusing your hygge on lightweight, breathable, cool clothing. **Choose shorts or shorter skirts so you can enjoy the feeling of the fresh air and breeze when you spend time outdoors. Pick tank tops and t-shirts, and bring along a light jacket or sweater for cooler nights. At this time of year, it can be fun to dress in bold, vibrant colors, so be sure you pick colors that make you feel comfortable, and happy when you look at them. As always, choose items for the comfort they can provide, instead of the current fashion trends**

Many people may feel pressured to wear fashionable swimsuits at this time of year. Remember hygge even when choosing your bathing suit! Pick something you feel comfortable in—physically as well as emotionally. Don't force yourself to wear something you wouldn't normally choose just because it may be what's in style this year.

HYGGE FALL CLOTHES

In the fall, look for clothes that feature warm hygge-friendly colors like brown, gray, and cream. You may still choose thinner fabrics at this time of the year, but you'll want to dress in layers so you can add or remove clothing as needed depending on the weather. You may also need to have a raincoat handy at this time of the year, so pick one that's comfortable to wear and doesn't make you feel overheated or weighed down too much when you have it on. Even though you may be tempted to wear stylish autumn boots, it's better to pick clothes for comfort, so keep this in mind when choosing your shoes at this time of year, too.

HYGGE WINTER CLOTHES

This is the time of year when your clothes can really incorporate the hygge lifestyle. Choose clothing items that make you feel warm and cozy inside and out. Go with soft, plush fabrics and be sure to wear a coat that's lined for extra comfort. Try wearing stockings or very thick socks with your outfits to keep your feet and legs warm and toasty when it's very cold outside. And don't neglect your hands and face! Wear gloves and a scarf and hat. For best results, try knitting or crocheting these items yourself, or wearing ones made by someone you love if you aren't able to make them.

CHAPTER 10:

HONORING HYGGE OUTSIDE OF THE HOME

Deciding to live the hygge lifestyle doesn't mean making your home your only place of comfort and staying there all the time. You can experience this Danish method of happiness anywhere you go. In fact, Danish vacations and family activities fall right into many of the principles you learned earlier in the book: ease, coziness, and togetherness. Picnics, short trips, and playing games are all a part of the Danish culture, as well. Peruse the list below for some additional ideas on how to incorporate hygge in all aspects of your life, including activities outside the home.

15 IDEAS FOR HYGGE ACTIVITIES

1. Cook a special meal together as a family. While this suggestion may seem like something you would only do within the home, you can actually make this happen on vacation as well. Rent a hotel room or a condo with a kitchen included, or go camping and cook your meal together over an open fire. There are many ways to cook with your family whether you're at home or not.

2. Play a board game or do a puzzle together. Just like cooking with your family, this activity is portable for any vacation or for fun in the comfort of your own home

3. Have a picnic in a quiet and serene place. Plan this excursion on your own or with people you care about. If you go on a picnic alone, be sure to tell someone where you'll be for safety purposes.

4. Take a family bike ride through the country or on a nearby beautiful trail. If you don't own bikes, you can often rent them for the day from bike stores.

5. Take a road trip and stop at one spot chosen by each family member. This may take some planning ahead of time. Ask the people in your family where they'd like to stop, and don't tease or laugh at the places they pick, even if some of them are not stops you would choose to make on your own. This practice will ensure everyone feels included equally.

6. Take a weekend camping trip. If you can't get away long enough for a longer camping vacation with your family, why not take a short camping trip over a weekend? You may also want to wait for a long weekend from school or work to plan this trip.

7. Travel somewhere where it snows and play in the snow together. Depending on where you live, it may be hard to find a place where it snows without having to travel by plane. If it's going to take extensive effort to take your family to a snowy place, this may be better suited as a winter vacation than a quick trip.

8. Enjoy hot chocolate by a fire and watch a family movie. Make this experience even more exciting by offering a hot chocolate toppings bar and letting everyone decorate their cocoa the way they want to. Plan to do this often and take turns choosing the movie so everyone is actively involved.

9. Go fishing together. Do you know how to fish? You might not, but even if you don't, you can learn along with your kids. There's no reason why this activity can't be a fun family experience, even if you don't know how to do it yourself. Be sure to check local laws and regulations before you head out.

10. Read a classic book as a family. You can either do this aloud or plan to read separately and then discuss the book together at a later time. Make this more hygge by going to the park and sitting in a quiet location while you all read together on the weekends. You may also be able to do this experience in the evenings after school while it's light enough outside.

11. Bake a dessert together. Just like cooking together, this can happen inside or outside the home. If you bake together inside the home, you may want to share your dessert with people in your community or with friends.

12. Go caroling together. If you're looking for a way to bring more hygge into your holidays, why not try caroling as a family? Be sure to practice this safely and do not go into strangers' homes while caroling.

13. Locate an open space and play a sport together. Whether it's the park, a community baseball field, a gym, or a beach volleyball net, try getting active and playing sports with your kids. They don't have to be formal games, and you can just play around together while spending time with each other.

14. If you have a dog, take it for a long walk and take note of all the animals, insects and plants you see. This is a great way to incorporate hygge with caring for your pets. You may also choose this time to teach your kids more about proper dog care, too.

15. Go on a short hike to a waterfall. If you live somewhere near hiking trails or walking paths, try taking one or more of these on weekends. Whether you're on your own, with friends, or with your whole family, hiking to a waterfall can give you a sense of peace and mindfulness while allowing you to experience nature's beauty.

HYGGE HOBBIES

A hygge hobby is anything that offers you stress relief and comfort. You should engage in hobbies that bring you into the present and allow you to forget your worries and stress. The more engaging and absorbing a hobby is, the more mindful it will make you!

Try some of the following hobbies to improve your hygge experience overall:

* Yoga. This practice can help you become more mindful and therefore more hygge.

* Jogging. By working on your health and getting outdoors more, you'll be enjoying hygge even more.

* Knitting, embroidering, and other crafts. Being creative as a hobby is a fun way to encourage your own self-expression. It can also be something fun you do in your personal space inside your home.

* Painting. This creative activity can be fun to do outdoors or inside.

* Hiking. Take an easy hike if you're not experienced, or go for a more strenuous one if you want to challenge yourself while still having a chance to get outside.

Anything you enjoy that can increase mindfulness is a good hobby to incorporate into your hygge lifestyle!

HYGGE AND TRAVEL

The Danish love to travel, and for good reason! Taking in the world around you and appreciating the experiences travel brings you is essential to being happy. If your budget allows, try to travel as much as you can. Although we've already talked a little about traveling at the holidays, this section can give you more in-depth tips about hygge travel plans.

Many Americans associate travel with stress. To be truly hygge about travel, you want to take it slow and enjoy your time abroad or wherever you may be visiting. Don't plan every moment, but instead allow experiences to happen as they will. Not everything needs to be perfect, and often plans fall apart, so don't expect to strictly follow a schedule. Instead, wake up each morning, decide what you want to do, and do it. Tailor experiences to your preferences.

With that said, you may feel stressed if you go into a vacation with zero plans. Make sure you at least plan for how you will get around your vacation destination and how you'll get back home when you're finished traveling. It's also a good idea to plan your hotel or other lodging ahead of time to reduce stress. After that, being spontaneous is much more relaxing.

You should also maximize your comfort. Bring a neck pillow on planes or long car rides, as well as a soft, plush blanket. When traveling by air, you'll be much more comfortable with noise-cancelling earplugs or headphones while on the plane. If traveling with children, bring plenty of comfort items for them as well. You should also plan to bring distractions for them, since they may get more restless than adults during long trips.

Many people fail to plan for a cold draft on planes or buses, so be sure to bring warm socks and a comfortable sweatshirt. Sleep when you can. You may consider bringing your own pillow and blanket to help you sleep in unfamiliar rooms. Bring the items you need to feel at home, such as hand sanitizer, a spray that smells like home, or headphones to listen to music that soothes you. While it is great to try new foods, you should also bring comfort foods that remind you of home in case your stomach doesn't agree with the foreign foods. Don't forget to bring any medications you might need for the duration of your trip so you aren't scrambling to find them in a strange place.

Be sure to stay within budget. There is nothing quite like financial insecurity to ruin the pleasure of travel. It's acceptable to stay at a budget hostel or motel instead of breaking the bank for a five-star hotel when you'll be out and about for most of the day anyway. Taking the train or bus can be cheaper and less stressful than driving. There is no need to splurge on first class when coach is perfectly functional. Find ways to save money and shop deals on sites like Travelzoo, Sherman's Travels or Scott's Cheap Flights.

Picking beautiful destinations is key. You want to enjoy traveling and enjoy the world around you. Experiencing new things and beautiful places will help you feel hygge immensely. Even if you can't afford to go overseas or far away from home, you can have many amazing experiences when you travel. Most people don't even realize how many unique sights there are near their own homes. With "staycations" becoming more and more popular for Americans, finding hidden gems near your hometown can be a great way to vacation without spending a lot of money. Why not look for "off the beaten path" locations near you? Find a few walking trails or other nature spots close by and stay in a cheap hotel room or campsite for a short but sweet getaway if you are unable to afford a bigger vacation.

No matter whether you plan to travel far away or stay close to home, the important hygge concept to keep in mind is expanding your horizons as well as your family's. Make new experiences for yourself and your family when you travel. Find out about cultures you may not know much about, and practice new languages. Discover the history of a location—even if it's your own town or region. And in all things, remain mindful, cozy, comfortable, and hygge. Taking a trip will help you feel peaceful and joyful in no time.

CHAPTER 11:
21 DAYS
OF HYGGE
CHALLENGE

Now that you have read up on the hygge lifestyle, we want to leave you with a challenge. This is a challenge to try 21 days of living with hygge in your heart. Think of it as slowly starting a diet. Try one new aspect of hygge each day. This way, you will not only ease into this new happy lifestyle and begin to see the changes it is making inside of you, but you can also find out which aspects of hygge work best for you. You can then plan to go forward.

So, it's time to go get a calendar and choose to try at least one thing each day. You could do this however you want—by increasing the number of things you do each day as the weeks go on, or just trying one brand new practice each of the 21 days. Get your family involved and have fun with it! You'll already be fulfilling the hygge principle of togetherness.

21 WAYS TO INCORPORATE HYGGE INTO YOUR DAILY LIFE

DAY ONE:

Set aside a night without screens and tech. Spend time with your friends and family talking, playing games, and bonding with each other.

DAY TWO:

Bake bread from scratch. If you have kids, let them help, too!

DAY THREE:

Bring something from outdoors inside (rocks, flowers, nature décor). Just be sure it's something safe to bring inside.

DAY FOUR:

Have a movie night with friends and family. Refer back to Day One and turn off your electronics during the movie for best results.

DAY FIVE:

Find a quiet, comfortable place and read a book in your at-home personal space.

DAY SIX:

Have a relaxing stay-in-your-pajamas day. If you have to work and can't make time for a whole day, try spending your free time after work in your pajamas instead.

DAY SEVEN:

Have breakfast in bed. Make it the night before, so you can grab it and return to bed to enjoy it.

DAY EIGHT:

Take a stroll through a park or nature preserve. If you don't live near either of these, take a walk outdoors anywhere.

DAY NINE:

Start a gratitude journal. Don't forget to pick a journal with a cover that brings you joy.

DAY TEN:

Use candlelight instead of electricity for a night. Play music as a family or read a book together during this time.

DAY ELEVEN:

Watch the sun rise or set, preferably with a loved one.

DAY TWELVE:

Have a warm drink at a quiet café with an old friend. Or, if you need some time to yourself to unwind, do this activity on your own instead. Be sure to bring a book so you're not glued to your electronics!

DAY THIRTEEN:

Have a hot chocolate night with the family. Have fun add-ins like marshmallows and sprinkles so everyone can make their cocoa special.

DAY FOURTEEN:

Give yourself an at-home spa day with natural scrubs and soaps. Pick soothing, rejuvenating essential oils.

DAY FIFTEEN:

Try beginner yoga. You can use videos from the internet and save money on an actual class at a studio!

DAY SIXTEEN:

Hug everyone you care about freely. Just be sure to give them a fair warning and don't startle them!

Day Seventeen:

Listen to calming music. If you do so while meditating, that's even better!

Day Eighteen:

Take a walk around the neighborhood in sweatpants and a comfortable shirt. Take time to feel the breeze and make note of the smells and sounds around you.

Day Nineteen:

Hold hands with your spouse or other loved one while watching a movie. Sit close to each other and enjoy each other's company.

Day Twenty:

Lay in bed and talk to someone, either on the phone or in person.

Day Twenty-One:

Color in an adult coloring book. Better yet, make it a family experience and have every one color together!

CHAPTER 12:

BEYOND THE 21
DAY CHALLENGE

Hygge does not just stop after you check off the activities on the above list. Once you practice the hygge lifestyle for three weeks, you won't want to return to your typical hectic and routine! You can take hygge beyond the 21 days challenge in the previous chapter and make it a permanent fixture of your life.

Remember that hygge is about living in the moment, so forcing it and worrying about how to achieve it is counterproductive. Instead, just make an effort to enjoy at least one moment of your day. Soon, this lifestyle will become such an ingrained habit that you won't even have to think about it. You will want to do it naturally, so it won't take any work on your part.

Make an effort to take care of yourself. Take a few minutes to relax at least once a day. You owe it to yourself to be more hygge in your attitude and your routine. Not every moment will be comfortable or enjoyable; you can't always forget about your worries and cares. But if you practice hygge mindfulness at least once a day, you will find a new enjoyment of life.

Also, make your home and workplace a hygge atmosphere. These measures will help you enjoy a more fulfilling life. When you change your décor and wardrobe to be more comfortable, you will have fewer distractions and irritations plaguing your day and ruining your mood

Try starting a new pleasant morning routine to set the mood for the present day. Don't watch upsetting news stories on TV or scroll through glamorous posts on social media that fill you with envy. Don't hit the ground running, already burning energy in a hectic dash to get out the door in time. Instead, enjoy yourself. Wake up early and do some yoga or sip some tea without a feeling of anxiety and panic. Enjoy a leisurely breakfast with your loved ones. Get ready and enjoy the physical sensations of showering, getting dressed, doing your hair, and applying makeup. Try to take in the sunrise and the birdsong of early morning.

Getting your friends and family on board can help you make your life more hygge as well. You can all enjoy the precious moments together while omitting distractions like phones and TV.

CONCLUSION:

EXTENDING YOUR HAPPINESS

As the title of the book, "The Danish Secrets of Happiness: How to Be Happy and Healthy in Your Daily Life," suggests, all this information is aimed at helping you find happiness in our currently chaotic world. It can be challenging to figure out what brings you true happiness, but this book is intended to provide you with the groundwork you need to get started. Happiness is something many of us, even in privileged societies, find ourselves chasing. However, the chase may be exactly what is making us unhappy. With hygge, you can slow down and find happiness and peace in the simple pleasures, which is a feeling that cannot be bought. Living the Danish way can be a rewarding experience for the whole family, so remember to be grateful and cozy and spend time together!

REVIEWS

Reviews and feedback help improve this book and the author. If you enjoy this book, we would greatly appreciate it if you could take a few moments to share your opinion and post a review on Amazon.

FREE BONUS
HYGGE GIFT IDEAS

Go to r68881zo.beget.tech to download the guide for free

Printed in Great Britain
by Amazon